Spirit of the Rock

Spirit of the Rock

RON KAUK

Gibbs Smith, Publisher

First Edition
07 06 05 04 03   5 4 3 2 1

Text copyright © 2003 by Ron Kauk
Photograph copyrights as noted on page 96

Published by
Gibbs Smith, Publisher
P.O. Box 667
Layton, Utah 84041

www.gibbs-smith.com
Orders 1-800-748-5439

Jacket design and art direction by Kurt Wahlner
Interior design by J. Scott Knudsen, Park City

Printed and bound in China

Printed on New Leaf Reincarnation paper:
100% recycled, 50% post-consumer waste,
processed chlorine-free.

By using New Leaf paper on this project, the
following resources have been saved:

14	trees
1,223	pounds of solid waste
1,346	gallons of water
1,755	kilowatt hours of electricity (2/3 months of electric power required by the average U.S. home)
2,223	pounds of greenhouse gases (1,800 miles equivalent driving the average American car)
10	pounds of HAPs, VOCs, and AOX combined
3	cubic yards of landfill space

**Library of Congress
Cataloging-in-Publication Data**

Kauk, Ron.
  Spirit of the rock / Ron Kauk.— 1st ed.
    p. cm.
  ISBN 1-58685-150-0
  1. Rock climbing. 1. Title.
GV200.2 .K38 2003
796.52'23—dc21
          2002152103

To the spirit of the rock that continues

to give those of us who choose to respect

it a way of life to discover the beauty,

mystery, and freedom to move in

harmony with the natural world.

In the lessons of the vertical world lies

the power of conscious connection to

spirit—in the rock, air, water, trees,

and each other.

Foreword

I like climbing with Ron. We both enjoy moving over good granite or gneiss with the least amount of gear. Keeping it simple.

We choose to believe that the granite is alive. If life is movement, then rock—with its atoms flying around like stars in the cosmos—is alive. It's a harmless concept that adds a lot of enjoyment and respect and responsibility to our lives.

—Yvon Chouinard
Ventura, California
October 24, 2002

Stopped by a Snowstorm

My friend and I wait at the entrance to the Yosemite Valley. He's sixteen years old with a new driver's license; I'm thirteen or fourteen. Looking out the window watching big snowflakes slowly falling, creating a white blanket over the oak and pine trees, boulders—everything except the river that flows so pure and clean, knowing where it wants to go. Everything is peaceful, so inviting.

The feeling is to open the door and run into this beautiful world where everything seems to have a place. In my young mind, contemplating physically doing this, the moment is so strong. I am mesmerized by believing that this place will take care of me, teach me to be happy and free. Like casting out a kind of dream into those woods.

Over thirty years later there's an understanding of that moment. The door did open and I ran into the natural world—the same one I truly am inside. I held onto this belief and it became a reality: Yosemite does take care of me, just like the earth takes care of all her people.

Letting the moves come to me feels better than forcing my way. Just let the moves come to you. Extend your spirit, not your ego.

A Beginner's Mind

Remembering a beginner's mind, a place free to move inside and outside of ourselves in full connection, with no real expectations, just pure adventure in seeing what's just beyond that next move. Moving in our environment and our minds to create a world balanced by challenge, respect, and responsibility that freedom always demands.

Climb to be free.

Bouldering in Camp 4

Freedom has so much to do with understanding our potential—finding the simplicity to move in our own rhythm, to feel the harmony of mind and body. Completely committed to the excitement and spirit of adventure to just do your best. Let the rest come to you.

Bouldering in Camp 4 in the '70s was all about going with the flow. Every move our climbing tribe was making, on or off the rock, seemed to be connected to each other and this sacred ground that's always an honor to be a part of. Even climbing Midnight Lightning wasn't just about the challenge to pull through the outrageous moves; it was always about the opportunity to be a part of this beautiful place.

Friends for Life

Jerry Moffatt, one of my best friends, from England, describes granite as the gods' rock. And this really comes through on Thriller, a slightly overhanging wall of smooth rock with beautifully carved selected holds that make their connection with you when the time is right. Just like finding a new friend, you know, like hanging out, getting to know someone, learning about yourself along the way, creating and sharing experiences.

Boulders are like old friends. If we find respect and honor each other we can all share a stronger, happier, healthier life.

Remembering

It's funny to think that words could even begin to explain all the days, years, moods, and seasons of climbing on this cliff, or describe all the different people climbing together or apart but still sharing the space. I hear the river and feel the sun warming us on a winter's day, or an afternoon breeze cooling us off in summer after swimming in the river below.

Climbing on the cliff is as good as it gets—solid rock surrounded by beautiful oaks, manzanita, bay trees, deer, lizards, ants, or the elusive bobcat. Directly across is Elephant Rock, home area for the mighty golden eagle. Blue sky, puffy white clouds . . . do you get the picture? It's heaven on earth.

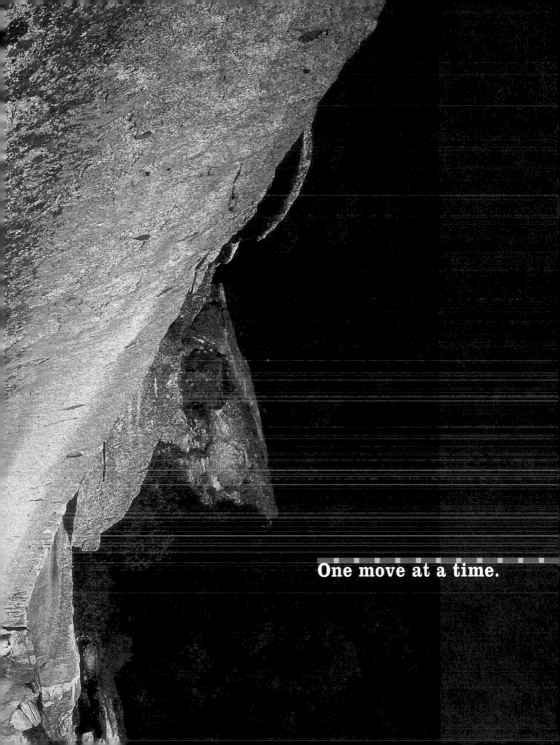

One move at a time.

Sacred Wind

Today the wind told me that the whole world is one country.

The wind is connected to everything as it blows across land and water. It told me that, in essence, all people are the same, and also connected to everything in nature's creation.

It's okay if you don't believe me. Next time you feel the wind, just ask it. See, the wind has been traveling the earth since long before you and me.

BUTTERFLY

Today I saw a beautiful butterfly.
It stopped and allowed me to gaze and
    wonder at the beauty of it,
Brown with turquoise spots all around
    the wings. So pretty, so free.
And it landed wherever it wanted to be.

This nature that's all around us has something
    to say.
It's real important for all of us to hear this today.
We need to take care of ourselves,
And in order to do this, we have to
    take care of nature.

It's a circle, it's a cycle, it's a way for life.
It's said over and over in every breath we take,
In every heartbeat,
Repeating over and over

Take care of nature and nature will take care of you.
Take care of nature and nature will take care of you.
Take care of nature and nature will take care of you.
Take care of nature and nature will take care of you.

If you get confused, sit back and look at the moon
    and the stars and ask yourself

How could it be so beautiful?

Call of the Warrior

In a time when we don't even stop to ask why, the most important thing is to climb, to search. It's as if do or die, our commitment to climb hard and everything in sight. Looking for new ways to take the lead in finding the way to the very hardest climbs of the day.

Tales of Power had its time, helping fulfill this destiny to fuel the fire that constantly pushed us. One day while climbing at Elephant Rock with my Australian friend Nick Taylor, we spotted a steep wall across the canyon that looked like it had a perfect crack running through it. Setting our sights on it, we said we'd have to check it out. It's funny to remember how we thrashed down Wildcat Creek, walked along steep granite slabs covered with grass and leaves, slippery stuff.

Nick the jokester got to the base before me and said, "Man, it's just a water streak, there's nothing." Surprised and let down, I walked to the base and looked up at this incredible climb with a perfect crack running up the colorful wall and very overhanging for Yosemite free climbing at the time. That moment's frozen in my mind.

Never let go of
your dreams.

Another opportunity provided by the natural wonders of rock. How many years had this wall been standing before two young guys strayed off the beaten path to look into the future of their potential, as what at the time felt like training to be some kind of warrior. See, these books that Carlos Castaneda had written became a kind of handbook to help guide some of us back to the magic and mystery of life that was never presented in public school. A very welcome chance to open our minds through the power within to connect with realms beyond the box, as they say now.

This was around 1977, after many big efforts learning how to fall, finally making it up this wall only to look up and see a twenty-foot horizontal roof. My mouth hung open.

Yeah, stacked right on top of Tales of Power waited the next step—Separate Reality. It's so amazing if we just commit with passion and the love to do something how the universe really will provide. That's my reflection—imagining now the incredible abundance there is to discover our dreams, whatever they may be.

Separate Reality

One of the best people I ever had the honor to know was Wolfgang Gullich, a German climber who told me the first time he saw a picture of Separate Reality was on the cover of *Mountain Magazine* in 1978. He said he was totally confused about which way to look at it and kept turning the magazine around and around. At that time, to climb a twenty-foot horizontal roof, hanging upside down, was basically unheard of. He said that for him and in his area it sparked a kind of free-climbing revolution, as young minds opened to what might be possible.

This twenty-foot horizontal climb required some serious training, which I was forced to do while trying to earn some money working for my dad digging house foundations with the old shovel that created new stomach muscles that I'm now sure were part of the secret to hanging upside down and spinning around at the lip feet first to pull over the top.

It's great to see how we can affect each other through inspiration and commitment to raise our level of ability, like Wolfgang took training and climbing to another level. (I still can't believe he climbed Separate Reality without a rope.) More importantly, he'll always shine for me as someone who understood how to be a good person as well as an inspiration for the climbing world.

Let go of
everything
but what you
need to stay
on the rock.

Hi, How's it Going?

Yes, I climb these rocks. It's true.
But it's not the only thing I do.
Living in a place like this
Is to discover bliss,
The kind that's so hard to miss.
If you're climbing so high
Heading for the sky
Or just walking through the woods
Diving in the river in summer
Or making a new friend to share and discover
In peaceful thought,
marveling at the beauty of the birds
Singing so happy and free, they seem to be
Flying from tree to tree
Always amazes me.
And I hope you too,
as we might pass each other by
And recognize this miracle in a simple way
Of just saying hi.

Astroman

Timing is such a wild story. We had such luck, fate, destiny to be the first ones to free climb this incredible wall.

Walking up to something as awesome as the East Face (Astroman) is a real experience anytime. Just observing those little swift birds doing their flying acrobatics and making that now so familiar cheet-cheet-cheet, deet-deet-deet, or however you hear it, they are totally at home. Ravens cruising by give their caw to also remind you. A small lizard sticks to the orange rock not moving, hoping you won't notice him.

As a teenager, Astroman represented to me the ultimate opportunity to challenge oneself on many levels. Mentally, physically, and, without a doubt, spiritually. At the time I might not have said spiritually, but more a feeling about the power of creation. Magic is the only word to describe it, climbing pitch after pitch of the most perfect, beautifully sculpted granite in the world. Every step of the way has your full attention, making use of every foothold, every jam, looking for everything available to make it first try.

Now I realize why we thought we could climb it: it's really all about the ones who came before, who inspired us to prepare ourselves—to develop the physical

Make the
connection.

strength and technique to enter the unknown with confidence and take care of ourselves in this environment.

Once again, nature tells the story. Everything is ultimately interdependent. One life form counting on the other so that we can move in a positive direction with all our relations.

IT TAKES TIME

Learning to do nothing would seem non-productive. But it is only when we allow ourselves to slow down, to stop, look, and listen, that we begin to understand that we're part of something that is way beyond just us.

It takes time to feel.

It takes time to sit and observe.

It takes time to see all the things happening.

Right now the clouds are floating by. The waterfall's thundering down. The river is flowing through the meadow. Wind is moving through the trees and grass. The sounds are all natural. This is medicine for the spirit. It takes time to hear the story.

Magic Line

When the rock is teacher and the humble student must live up to the lesson—this was one of those challenges. Shedding layers to find your own core, a place where only truth lives. I must have spent about a year, on and off, trying to cross this magic line.

This is the most beautiful place on earth. Watching the maple tree grow leaves and then lose them. The waterfall change from raging to being frozen still. Try and try I did to cross over the wall between myself and

Accept the
process.

this climb. Learning to accept the process was the key. Every day there, I was learning more. But at the time, I didn't really know that no matter what, it's always an opportunity to grow. The beauty of this special lesson was learning to let go, freeing my mind and simply allowing my heart to find the love for the move and lead me to the core of my own truth.

I love to climb!

Find your place
with nature.

Slowing Down with the Oaks

I found a place in this tree. All it wants to do is help me. I climb into this special space, held by the tree, with water running all around. It's nature's surround sound filling me in a way that makes me relax and simply flow with all the elements. I am in connection with everything on the land. It's like going to have your battery recharged, reduce stress, or even more importantly, getting a dose of preventative medicine to live healthier and happier. At least that's how it feels to me. You could try it, too; just tell the oak that your friend Ron recommended you.

Sense of Place

I could never feel alone here. Just walking into this area feels so comfortable, like going to a special place in your house. I've been familiar with the sounds of the birds singing, wind in the trees, and a little frog that lives on the traverse who I hear but never see. There's a boulder that looks like a seat. It's a chair for me, this block of granite. I look north and see 12,000-foot High Sierra peaks. I've become accustomed to the light. In the foreground an old lodgepole pine turns golden in the afternoon.

Even though I have been bouldering here for years, it is a place I could never tire of. It is always interesting

Keep it sacred.

to continue to evolve within myself, check my ego, and let go of any kind of competitiveness or jealousy—the kind of stuff that might get in my way.

I want to be as honest as I can to understand why I love to just go back and forth along this rock. This place has given me so much education about moving in the moment without judgment or expectation, just trying to feel my way with the joy to move and relax. Good energy flows through my mind and body, whether it is one or two moves or traversing for ten laps.

Trying to connect to the moment, that move, that breath—this is what I have been striving for; finding the oneness that can exist with all the things around and inside me. Probably just like the little birds that always seem to be watching from their trees and the frog who knows his place too.

Make friends with the rock.

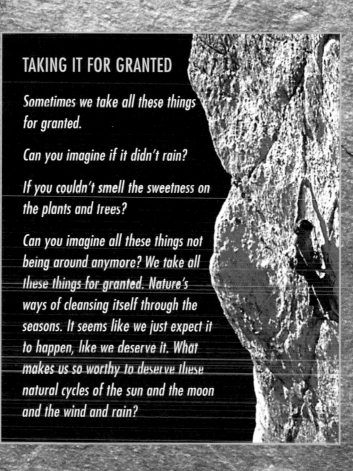

TAKING IT FOR GRANTED

Sometimes we take all these things for granted.

Can you imagine if it didn't rain?

If you couldn't smell the sweetness on the plants and trees?

Can you imagine all these things not being around anymore? We take all these things for granted. Nature's ways of cleansing itself through the seasons. It seems like we just expect it to happen, like we deserve it. What makes us so worthy to deserve these natural cycles of the sun and the moon and the wind and rain?

Getting Inside the Move

It came to me the other day while warming up to go climbing with a friend. We began to share the idea of feeling the moves we were making. For example, on a four-move boulder we would make one move and stay on that move long enough to feel what was going on, trying to recognize each point of contact, relaxing the mind to a point in order to focus on the feeling of the body hanging on with only what was needed, then let go, rest, and start again. Continue to the next move, come down, and repeat the process to the top or however it felt right.

This way was very interesting for me—to achieve what I now refer to as making a conscious connection with the mind, body, and rock. The conscious connection required slowing way down in order to better comprehend the action involved in a move. Opening the mind to remember how to practice something, not just trying to prove, compete, or conquer.

On the contrary, to develop our other senses—to feel from the inside out, extending our spirit to the spirit of the rock. My rating for that arrives at one of the highest levels possible for rock climbing and the winner gets all the joy, happiness, and freedom anyone could ever ask for. Did I mention peace and harmony as well?

The true beauty of the conscious connection is through lots of practice. I feel we could carry this over to driving a car, visiting with friends, eating our food, breathing air, drinking water, living in the sacred moment. And then maybe the ultimate connection, we could return to earth, becoming spiritually grounded and simply be happy.

How cool would that be?

(Please slow down and read this again, and remember to breathe from the diaphragm.)

Sacred World

Climbing has saved my life from the confines of the materialistic illusion we're taught as children in school. The way I see it, there are two worlds: the world where nothing is sacred except money, and the other world, where everything is sacred.

Living on
the earth is
one thing.
Living with
the earth is
another.

Sacred Granite

It amazes me to realize how sacred granite is, what it has provided—from sculptured works of art to the offering of a way of life.

The opportunity to write ourselves into these boulders and granite walls has created stories that can help us understand who we are. Thousands of people from around the world have come here to test themselves in this kind of initiation into the vertical world. Learning skills to overcome obstacles that become symbols of life's journey in general.

What a teacher the school of granite has been. At this point it's crazy for me to imagine life without granite, or any rock for that matter. That's why it feels so sacred. The sacredness of other things like air and water has become much clearer. So sacred are they that we can't live without them.

Isn't it amazing how everything is connected, or am I just easily amazed?

Move into balance.

El Capitan

I could never imagine conquering such a phenomenon as Grandfather El Capitan—three thousand feet of rock spirit. For me, maybe the most sacred of vertical journeys in the world, maybe the universe. Imagine that.

It's unbelievable to be hanging days on end, in a world stripped down to the basics: food, water, shelter, and skills to survive the day or whatever might come your way—wind, rain, snow, heat—being so vulnerable that there seems to be an ongoing rhythm of connection, like having your hand on the earth's pulse.

So aware, or beware, the natural laws are always there.

Respect
the rock.

Sacred Water

Today I've learned, or should I say remembered, that the natural world is our most valuable gift— the sun, moon, land, air, and water. Nothing we do will ever rival the profound gifts of nature. Our job is to be responsible for these gifts for generations to come. The river told me this while I was observing, listening, feeling. Today this thought seemed as real as the water around—and inside me—where rivers are flowing as nature intended.

**Remember
the source.**

GETTING WATER

When I come here to get my water, I try not to just take it, but give thanks for it and observe it, listen to it. Really think and feel about what it has to say in relation to the story of life and creation.

My little friends, these birds, when they sit and sing in their trees and look around, I think to myself, "This wouldn't be the same without you. Thank you for sharing your world with me."

Oneness

When we find oneness with the natural world, things like loneliness, jealousy, and greediness start to go away, and a kind of harmony comes into our lives that will nurture our spirit and help us live with love and compassion for all living things. Creating a world with equality and respect so the wheel of life can turn in a good way into the future.

Get Real!

Getting back to what is real in the sense of our life source is vital at this point in our history, just like in our climbing world. Where did we come from, what are our roots, what about stories and experiences of the first El Cap climbs?

A high level of commitment should always be a part of the experience. It is interesting to consider what this means when El Cap has been climbed a thousand times. It feels as though this idea of commitment must remain in the spirit of adventure, to discover who and what we are. Even better, perhaps, is what we can become in balance with the natural world.

Respect the Earth

A new beginning is the next step—a way back to the basics, our foundation with the earth. This is what is so great about the vertical world—there is never a doubt about where we are, we're hanging on for dear life with the ability to understand the natural laws of gravity. This is profound for me personally because if we don't obey this very simple truth, life could change or vanish in a moment's time. Can you believe it?

I hope our judgment can remain sane and always respect gravity. Climbing and the rock are incredible teachers about nature and the nature of us. So let's bring our experience of the vertical world to the realm of everyday life, and help each other make the world a better place through our actions. It's time for all of us to accept some sense of stewardship for our local areas, to protect and preserve the spirit of the rock and all of nature that provides us a life worth living.

With great appreciation and strong support for my Native American brothers and sisters, and all human beings who carry the truth in their hearts of how to respect our mother earth and each other through spirit. To all my relations.

—Ron Kauk

AS AN AMBASSADOR FOR PATAGONIA, RON HAS HELPED DEFINE THE CLIMBING LIFESTYLE AND POTENTIAL OF LIVES LIVED OUTSIDE. A PIONEER AND LEADER IN THE OUTDOOR CLOTHING BUSINESS, PATAGONIA HAS WORKED FOR ENVIRONMENTAL AND PROGRESSIVE SOCIAL CHANGE FOR THIRTY YEARS. TOGETHER RON AND PATAGONIA SHARE A VISION FOR THE FUTURE, FOR SUSTAINABLE LIFESTYLES AND COMMUNITIES THAT ABOVE ALL, RESPECT THE EARTH.

VISIT WWW.PATAGONIA.COM/SPIRIT FOR MORE INFORMATION ON PATAGONIA ENVIRONMENTAL PROGRAMS AND WAYS YOU CAN MAKE A DIFFERENCE IN YOUR COMMUNITY.

Photographic Credits

Phil Bard, 25, 33, 56
Mark Chapman, 35, 39
Greg Epperson, 8, 61, 74, 76
Chris Falkenstein, 4-5, 15, 22, 23, 24, 30, 31, 38, 40, 41, 42, 43, 57, 58, 60, 62, 63, 64, 65,67, 69, 71, 72-73, 77, 83, 84, 85, 89, 90-91, 92-93
Josh Helling, 2, 10-11, 26-27, 57, 79, 80, 82
Mike Hoover, 16, 18, 37
Ron Kauk, 48, 59, 86
Ron Kauk Collection, 10-11, 12-13, 14, 49, 81
Shawn Reeder, 20-21, 87
Galen Rowell, 17, 45, 46, 47, 95
Jim Thornburg, 7, 28, 50, 51, 52, 53, 54, 55
Kevin Worrall, 70
Heinz Zak, 37